AUGURIES OF INNOCENCE
AND
OTHER LYRIC POEMS

WILLIAM BLAKE

ISBN: 978-1495380877

Table of Contents

Auguries of Innocence

To see a World in a Grain of Sand
And a Heaven in a wild flower,
Hold Infinity in the palm of your hand
And Eternity in an hour.
A Robin redbreast in a Cage
Puts all Heaven in a Rage.
A dove house fill'd with doves & Pigeons
Shudders Hell thro' all its regions.
A dog starv'd at his Master's Gate
Predicts the ruin of the State.
A Horse misus'd upon the Road
Calls to Heaven for Human blood.
Each outcry of the hunted Hare
A fibre from the Brain does tear.
A Skylark wounded in the wing,
A Cherubim does cease to sing.
The Game Cock clipp'd and arm'd for fight
Does the Rising sun affright.
Every Wolf's & Lion's howl
Raises from Hell a Human Soul.
The wild deer, wand'ring here & there,
Keeps the Human Soul from Care.
The Lamb misus'd breeds public strife
And yet forgives the Butcher's Knife.
The Bat that flits at close of Eve
Has left the Brain that won't believe.
The Owl that calls upon the Night
Speaks the Unbeliever's fright.
He who shall hurt the little Wren
Shall never be belov'd by Men.
He who the Ox to wrath has mov'd
Shall never be by Woman lov'd.
The wanton Boy that kills the Fly
Shall feel the Spider's enmity.
He who torments the Chafer's sprite
Weaves a Bower in endless night.
The Catterpillar on the Leaf

Repeats to thee thy Mother's grief.
Kill not the Moth nor Butterfly,
For the Last Judgement draweth nigh.
He who shall train the Horse to War
Shall never pass the Polar Bar.
The Beggar's Dog & Widow's Cat,
Feed them & thou wilt grow fat.
The Gnat that sings his Summer's song
Poison gets from Slander's tongue.
The poison of the Snake & Newt
Is the sweat of Envy's Foot.
The poison of the Honey Bee
Is the Artist's Jealousy.
The Prince's Robes & Beggars' Rags
Are Toadstools on the Miser's Bags.
A truth that's told with bad intent
Beats all the Lies you can invent.
It is right it should be so;
Man was made for Joy & Woe;
And when this we rightly know
Thro' the World we safely go.
Joy & Woe are woven fine,
A Clothing for the Soul divine;
Under every grief & pine
Runs a joy with silken twine.
The Babe is more than swadling Bands;
Throughout all these Human Lands
Tools were made, & born were hands,
Every Farmer Understands.
Every Tear from Every Eye
Becomes a Babe in Eternity.
This is caught by Females bright
And return'd to its own delight.
The Bleat, the Bark, Bellow & Roar
Are Waves that Beat on Heaven's Shore.
The Babe that weeps the Rod beneath
Writes Revenge in realms of death.
The Beggar's Rags, fluttering in Air,
Does to Rags the Heavens tear.

The Soldier arm'd with Sword & Gun,
Palsied strikes the Summer's Sun.
The poor Man's Farthing is worth more
Than all the Gold on Afric's Shore.
One Mite wrung from the Labrer's hands
Shall buy & sell the Miser's lands:
Or, if protected from on high,
Does that whole Nation sell & buy.
He who mocks the Infant's Faith
Shall be mock'd in Age & Death.
He who shall teach the Child to Doubt
The rotting Grave shall ne'er get out.
He who respects the Infant's faith
Triumph's over Hell & Death.
The Child's Toys & the Old Man's Reasons
Are the Fruits of the Two seasons.
The Questioner, who sits so sly,
Shall never know how to Reply.
He who replies to words of Doubt
Doth put the Light of Knowledge out.
The Strongest Poison ever known
Came from Caesar's Laurel Crown.
Nought can deform the Human Race
Like the Armour's iron brace.
When Gold & Gems adorn the Plow
To peaceful Arts shall Envy Bow.
A Riddle or the Cricket's Cry
Is to Doubt a fit Reply.
The Emmet's Inch & Eagle's Mile
Make Lame Philosophy to smile.
He who Doubts from what he sees
Will ne'er believe, do what you Please.
If the Sun & Moon should doubt
They'd immediately Go out.
To be in a Passion you Good may do,
But no Good if a Passion is in you,
The Whore & Gambler, by the State
Licenc'd, build that Nation's Fate.
The Harlot's cry from Street to Street

Shall weave Old England's winding Sheet.
The Winner's Shout, the Loser's Curse,
Dance before dead England's Hearse.
Every Night & every Morn
Some to Misery are Born.
Every Morn & every Night
Some are Born to sweet Delight.
Some ar Born to sweet Delight,
Some are born to Endless Night.
We are led to Believe a Lie
When we see not Thro' the Eye
Which was Born in a Night to Perish in a Night
When the Soul Slept in Beams of Light.
God Appears & God is Light
To those poor Souls who dwell in the Night,
But does a Human Form Display
To those who Dwell in Realms of day.

Jerusalem/And Did Those Feet in Ancient Time

And did those feet in ancient time
Walk upon England's mountains green?
And was the holy Lamb of God
On England's pleasant pastures seen?

And did the Countenance Divine
Shine forth upon our clouded hills?
And was Jerusalem builded here
Among these dark satanic mills?

Bring me my bow of burning gold!
Bring me my arrows of desire!
Bring me my spear! O clouds, unfold!
Bring me my chariot of fire!

I will not cease from mental fight,
Nor shall my sword sleep in my hand,

Till we have built Jerusalem
In England's green and pleasant land.

Broken Love

My Spectre around me night and day
Like a wild beast guards my way;
My Emanation far within
Weeps incessantly for my sin.

'A fathomless and boundless deep,
There we wander, there we weep;
On the hungry craving wind
My Spectre follows thee behind.

'He scents thy footsteps in the snow
Wheresoever thou dost go,
Thro' the wintry hail and rain.
When wilt thou return again?

'Dost thou not in pride and scorn
Fill with tempests all my morn,
And with jealousies and fears
Fill my pleasant nights with tears?

'Seven of my sweet loves thy knife
Has bereavèd of their life.
Their marble tombs I built with tears,
And with cold and shuddering fears.

'Seven more loves weep night and day
Round the tombs where my loves lay,
And seven more loves attend each night
Around my couch with torches bright.

'And seven more loves in my bed
Crown with wine my mournful head,
Pitying and forgiving all
Thy transgressions great and small.

'When wilt thou return and view
My loves, and them to life renew?
When wilt thou return and live?
When wilt thou pity as I forgive?'

'O'er my sins thou sit and moan:
Hast thou no sins of thy own?
O'er my sins thou sit and weep,
And lull thy own sins fast asleep.

'What transgressions I commit
Are for thy transgressions fit.
They thy harlots, thou their slave;
And my bed becomes their grave.

'Never, never, I return:
Still for victory I burn.
Living, thee alone I'll have;
And when dead I'll be thy grave.

'Thro' the Heaven and Earth and Hell
Thou shalt never, quell:
I will fly and thou pursue:
Night and morn the flight renew.'

'Poor, pale, pitiable form
That I follow in a storm;
Iron tears and groans of lead
Bind around my aching head.

'Till I turn from Female love
And root up the Infernal Grove,
I shall never worthy be
To step into Eternity.

'And, to end thy cruel mocks,
Annihilate thee on the rocks,
And another form create

To be subservient to my fate.

'Let us agree to give up love,
And root up the Infernal Grove;
Then shall we return and see
The worlds of happy Eternity.

'And throughout all Eternity
I forgive you, you forgive me.
As our dear Redeemer said:
"This the Wine, and this the Bread."'

A Song

Sweet dreams, form a shade
O'er my lovely infant's head!
Sweet dreams of pleasant streams
By happy, silent, moony beams!

Sweet Sleep, with soft down
Weave thy brows an infant crown
Sweet Sleep, angel mild,
Hover o'er my happy child!

Sweet smiles, in the night
Hover over my delight!
Sweet smiles, mother's smile,
All the livelong night beguile.

Sweet moans, dovelike sighs,
Chase not slumber from thine eyes!
Sweet moan, sweeter smile,
All the dovelike moans beguile.

Sleep, sleep, happy child!
All creation slept and smiled.
Sleep, sleep, happy sleep,
While o'er thee doth mother weep.

Sweet babe, in thy face
Holy image I can trace;
Sweet babe, once like thee
Thy Maker lay, and wept for me:

Wept for me, for thee, for all,
When He was an infant small.
Thou His image ever see,
Heavenly face that smiles on thee!

Smiles on thee, on me, on all,
Who became an infant small;
Infant smiles are his own smiles;
Heaven and earth to peace beguiles.

Day

The Sun arises in the East,
Cloth'd in robes of blood and gold;
Swords and spears and wrath increase
All around his bosom roll'd
Crown'd with warlike fires and raging desires

A War Song to Englishmen

Prepare, prepare the iron helm of war,
Bring forth the lots, cast in the spacious orb;
Th' Angel of Fate turns them with mighty hands,
And casts them out upon the darken'd earth!
Prepare, prepare!

Prepare your hearts for Death's cold hand! prepare
Your souls for flight, your bodies for the earth;
Prepare your arms for glorious victory;
Prepare your eyes to meet a holy God!
Prepare, prepare!

Whose fatal scroll is that? Methinks 'tis mine!

Why sinks my heart, why faltereth my tongue?
Had I three lives, I'd die in such a cause,
And rise, with ghosts, over the well-fought field.
Prepare, prepare!

The arrows of Almighty God are drawn!
Angels of Death stand in the louring heavens!
Thousands of souls must seek the realms of light,
And walk together on the clouds of heaven!
Prepare, prepare!

Soldiers, prepare! Our cause is Heaven's cause;
Soldiers, prepare! Be worthy of our cause:
Prepare to meet our fathers in the sky:
Prepare, O troops, that are to fall to-day!
Prepare, prepare!

Alfred shall smile, and make his harp rejoice;
The Norman William, and the learnèd Clerk,
And Lion Heart, and black-brow'd Edward, with
His loyal queen, shall rise, and welcome us!
Prepare, prepare!

England! awake! awake! awake!

England! awake! awake! awake!
Jerusalem thy Sister calls!
Why wilt thou sleep the sleep of death
And close her from thy ancient walls?

Thy hills and valleys felt her feet
Gently upon their bosoms move:
Thy gates beheld sweet Zion's ways:
Then was a time of joy and love.

And now the time returns again:
Our souls exult, and London's towers
Receive the Lamb of God to dwell
In England's green and pleasant bowers.

An Imitation of Spenser

Golden Apollo, that thro' heaven wide
Scatter'st the rays of light, and truth's beams,
In lucent words my darkling verses dight,
And wash my earthy mind in thy clear streams,
That wisdom may descend in fairy dreams,
All while the jocund hours in thy train
Scatter their fancies at thy poet's feet;
And when thou yields to night thy wide domain,
Let rays of truth enlight his sleeping brain.
For brutish Pan in vain might thee assay
With tinkling sounds to dash thy nervous verse,
Sound without sense; yet in his rude affray,
(For ignorance is Folly's leasing nurse
And love of Folly needs none other's curse)
Midas the praise hath gain'd of lengthen'd ears,
For which himself might deem him ne'er the worse
To sit in council with his modern peers,
And judge of tinkling rimes and elegances terse.

And thou, Mercurius, that with wingèd brow
Dost mount aloft into the yielding sky,
And thro' Heav'n's halls thy airy flight dost throw,
Entering with holy feet to where on high
Jove weighs the counsel of futurity;
Then, laden with eternal fate, dost go
Down, like a falling star, from autumn sky,
And o'er the surface of the silent deep dost fly:
If thou arrivest at the sandy shore
Where nought but envious hissing adders dwell,
Thy golden rod, thrown on the dusty floor,
Can charm to harmony with potent spell.
Such is sweet Eloquence, that does dispel
Envy and Hate that thirst for human gore;
And cause in sweet society to dwell
Vile savage minds that lurk in lonely cell
O Mercury, assist my lab'ring sense
That round the circle of the world would fly,

As the wing'd eagle scorns the tow'ry fence
Of Alpine hills round his high aëry,
And searches thro' the corners of the sky,
Sports in the clouds to hear the thunder's sound,
And see the wingèd lightnings as they fly;
Then, bosom'd in an amber cloud, around
Plumes his wide wings, and seeks Sol's palace high.

And thou, O warrior maid invincible,
Arm'd with the terrors of Almighty Jove,
Pallas, Minerva, maiden terrible,
Lov'st thou to walk the peaceful solemn grove,
In solemn gloom of branches interwove?
Or bear'st thy aegis o'er the burning field,
Where, like the sea, the waves of battle move?
Or have thy soft piteous eyes beheld
The weary wanderer thro' the desert rove?
Or does th' afflicted man thy heav'nly bosom move?

Love and Harmony

Love and harmony combine,
And round our souls entwine
While thy branches mix with mine,
And our roots together join.

Joys upon our branches sit,
Chirping loud and singing sweet;
Like gentle streams beneath our feet
Innocence and virtue meet.

Thou the golden fruit dost bear,
I am clad in flowers fair;
Thy sweet boughs perfume the air,
And the turtle buildeth there.

There she sits and feeds her young,
Sweet I hear her mournful song;

And thy lovely leaves among,
There is love, I hear his tongue.

There his charming nest doth lay,
There he sleeps the night away;
There he sports along the day,
And doth among our branches play.

Love's Secret

Never seek to tell thy love,
Love that never told can be;
For the gentle wind does move
Silently, invisibly.

I told my love, I told my love,
I told her all my heart;
Trembling, cold, in ghastly fears,
Ah! she did depart!

Soon as she was gone from me,
A traveler came by,
Silently, invisibly
He took her with a sigh.

Mad Song

The wild winds weep
And the night is a-cold;
Come hither, Sleep,
And my griefs infold:
But lo! the morning peeps
Over the eastern steeps,
And the rustling birds of dawn
The earth do scorn.

Lo! to the vault
Of paved heaven,
With sorrow fraught

My notes are driven:
They strike the ear of night,
Make weep the eyes of day;
They make mad the roaring winds,
And with tempests play.

Like a fiend in a cloud,
With howling woe,
After night I do crowd,
And with night will go;
I turn my back to the east,
From whence comforts have increas'd;
For light doth seize my brain
With frantic pain.

Mock On, Mock On, Voltaire, Rousseau

Mock on, mock on, Voltaire, Rousseau;
Mock on, mock on; 'tis all in vain!
You throw the sand against the wind,
And the wind blows it back again.
And every sand becomes a gem
Reflected in the beams divine;
Blown back they blind the mocking eye,
But still in Israel's paths they shine.

The Atoms of Democritus
And Newton's Particles of Light
Are sands upon the Red Seashore,
Where Israel's tents do shine so bright.

Now Art Has Lost Its Mental Charms

'Now Art has lost its mental charms
France shall subdue the world in arms.'
So spoke an Angel at my birth;
Then said 'Descend thou upon earth,
Renew the Arts on Britain's shore,
And France shall fall down and adore.

With works of art their armies meet
And War shall sink beneath thy feet.
But if thy nation Arts refuse,
And if they scorn the immortal Muse,
France shall the arts of peace restore
And save thee from the ungrateful shore.'

Spirit who lov'st Britannia's Isle
Round which the fiends of commerce smile --

The Wild Flower's Song

As I wandered the forest,
The green leaves among,
I heard a Wild Flower
Singing a song.

'I slept in the earth
In the silent night,
I murmured my fears
And I felt delight.

'In the morning I went
As rosy as morn,
To seek for new joy;
But oh! met with scorn.'

Three Things to Remember

A Robin Redbreast in a cage,
Puts all Heaven in a rage.

A skylark wounded on the wing
Doth make a cherub cease to sing.

He who shall hurt the little wren
Shall never be beloved by men.

To Autumn

O Autumn, laden with fruit, and stainèd
With the blood of the grape, pass not, but sit
Beneath my shady roof; there thou may'st rest,
And tune thy jolly voice to my fresh pipe,
And all the daughters of the year shall dance!
Sing now the lusty song of fruits and flowers.
'The narrow bud opens her beauties to
The sun, and love runs in her thrilling veins;
Blossoms hang round the brows of Morning, and
Flourish down the bright cheek of modest Eve,
Till clust'ring Summer breaks forth into singing,
And feather'd clouds strew flowers round her head.

'The spirits of the air live on the smells
Of fruit; and Joy, with pinions light, roves round
The gardens, or sits singing in the trees.'
Thus sang the jolly Autumn as he sat;
Then rose, girded himself, and o'er the bleak
Hills fled from our sight; but left his golden load.

To Winter

O Winter! bar thine adamantine doors:
The north is thine; there hast thou built thy dark
Deep-founded habitation. Shake not thy roofs,
Nor bend thy pillars with thine iron car.'
He hears me not, but o'er the yawning deep
Rides heavy; his storms are unchain'd, sheathèd
In ribbèd steel; I dare not lift mine eyes,
For he hath rear'd his sceptre o'er the world.

Lo! now the direful monster, whose skin clings
To his strong bones, strides o'er the groaning rocks:
He withers all in silence, and in his hand
Unclothes the earth, and freezes up frail life.

He takes his seat upon the cliffs,--the mariner

Cries in vain. Poor little wretch, that deal'st
With storms!--till heaven smiles, and the monster
Is driv'n yelling to his caves beneath mount Hecla.

To Spring

O thou with dewy locks, who lookest down
Thro' the clear windows of the morning, turn
Thine angel eyes upon our western isle,
Which in full choir hails thy approach, O Spring!

The hills tell each other, and the listening
Valleys hear; all our longing eyes are turned
Up to thy bright pavilions: issue forth,
And let thy holy feet visit our clime.

Come o'er the eastern hills, and let our winds
Kiss thy perfumed garments; let us taste
Thy morn and evening breath; scatter thy pearls
Upon our love-sick land that mourns for thee.

O deck her forth with thy fair fingers; pour
Thy soft kisses on her bosom; and put
Thy golden crown upon her languished head,
Whose modest tresses were bound up for thee.

To Summer

O thou who passest thro' our valleys in
Thy strength, curb thy fierce steeds, allay the heat
That flames from their large nostrils! thou, O Summer,
Oft pitched'st here thy goldent tent, and oft
Beneath our oaks hast slept, while we beheld
With joy thy ruddy limbs and flourishing hair.

Beneath our thickest shades we oft have heard
Thy voice, when noon upon his fervid car
Rode o'er the deep of heaven; beside our springs
Sit down, and in our mossy valleys, on

Some bank beside a river clear, throw thy
Silk draperies off, and rush into the stream:
Our valleys love the Summer in his pride.

Our bards are fam'd who strike the silver wire:
Our youth are bolder than the southern swains:
Our maidens fairer in the sprightly dance:
We lack not songs, nor instruments of joy,
Nor echoes sweet, nor waters clear as heaven,
Nor laurel wreaths against the sultry heat.

To Nobodaddy

Why art thou silent & invisible
Father of jealousy
Why dost thou hide thyself in clouds
From every searching Eye

Why darkness & obscurity
In all thy words & laws
That none dare eat the fruit but from
The wily serpents jaws
Or is it because Secresy
gains females loud applause

A Grain of Sand

To see a world in a grain of sand,
And a heaven in a wild flower,
Hold infinity in the palm of your hand
And eternity in an hour.

To The Accuser Who is The God of This World

Truly My Satan thou art but a Dunce
And dost not know the Garment from the Man
Every Harlot was a Virgin once

Nor canst thou ever change Kate into Nan

Tho thou art Worship'd by the Names Divine
Of Jesus & Jehovah thou art still
The Son of Morn in weary Nights decline
The lost Travellers Dream under the Hill

To the Evening Star

Thou fair-haired angel of the evening,
Now, whilst the sun rests on the mountains, light
Thy bright torch of love; thy radiant crown
Put on, and smile upon our evening bed!
Smile on our loves, and while thou drawest the
Blue curtains of the sky, scatter thy silver dew
On every flower that shuts its sweet eyes
In timely sleep. Let thy west wind sleep on
The lake; speak silence with thy glimmering eyes,
And wash the dusk with silver. Soon, full soon,
Dost thou withdraw; then the wolf rages wide,
And the lion glares through the dun forest.
The fleeces of our flocks are covered with
Thy sacred dew; protect with them with thine influence.

To the Muses

Whether on Ida's shady brow,
Or in the chambers of the East,
The chambers of the sun, that now
From ancient melody have ceas'd;

Whether in Heav'n ye wander fair,
Or the green corners of the earth,
Or the blue regions of the air,
Where the melodious winds have birth;

Whether on crystal ye rove,
Beneath the bosom of the sea

Wand'ring in many a coral grove,
Fair Nine, forsaking Poetry!

How have you left the ancient love
That bards of old enjoy'd in you!
The languid strings do scarcely move!
The sound is forc'd, the notes are few!

To Thomas Butts

To my friend Butts I write
My first vision of light,
On the yellow sands sitting.
The sun was emitting
His glorious beams
From Heaven's high streams.
Over sea, over land,
My eyes did expand
Into regions of air,
Away from all care;
Into regions of fire,
Remote from desire;
The light of the morning
Heaven's mountains adorning:
In particles bright,
The jewels of light
Distinct shone and clear.
Amaz'd and in fear
I each particle gazèd,
Astonish'd, amazèd;
For each was a Man
Human-form'd. Swift I ran,
For they beckon'd to me,
Remote by the sea,
Saying: 'Each grain of sand,
Every stone on the land,
Each rock and each hill,
Each fountain and rill,

Each herb and each tree,
Mountain, hill, earth, and sea,
Cloud, meteor, and star,
Are men seen afar.'
I stood in the streams
Of Heaven's bright beams,
And saw Felpham sweet
Beneath my bright feet,
In soft Female charms;
And in her fair arms
My Shadow I knew,
And my wife's Shadow too,
And my sister, and friend.
We like infants descend
In our Shadows on earth,
Like a weak mortal birth.
My eyes, more and more,
Like a sea without shore,
Continue expanding,
The Heavens commanding;
Till the jewels of light,
Heavenly men beaming bright,
Appear'd as One Man,
Who complacent began
My limbs to enfold
In His beams of bright gold;
Like dross purg'd away
All my mire and my clay.
Soft consum'd in delight,
In His bosom sun-bright
I remain'd. Soft He smil'd,
And I heard His voice mild,
Saying: 'This is My fold,
O thou ram horn'd with gold,
Who awakest from sleep
On the sides of the deep.
On the mountains around
The roarings resound
Of the lion and wolf,

The loud sea, and deep gulf.
These are guards of My fold,
O thou ram horn'd with gold!'
And the voice faded mild;
I remain'd as a child;
All I ever had known
Before me bright shone:
I saw you and your wife
By the fountains of life.
Such the vision to me
Appear'd on the sea.

When Klopstock England Defied

When Klopstock England defied,
Uprose William Blake in his pride;
For old Nobodaddy aloft
Farted and belch'd and cough'd;
Then swore a great oath that made Heaven quake,
And call'd aloud to English Blake.
Blake was giving his body ease,
At Lambeth beneath the poplar trees.
From his seat then started he
And turn'd him round three times three.
The moon at that sight blush'd scarlet red,
The stars threw down their cups and fled,
And all the devils that were in hell,

Answerèd with a ninefold yell.
Klopstock felt the intripled turn,
And all his bowels began to churn,
And his bowels turn'd round three times three,
And lock'd in his soul with a ninefold key; . . .
Then again old Nobodaddy swore
He ne'er had seen such a thing before,
Since Noah was shut in the ark,
Since Eve first chose her hellfire spark,

Since 'twas the fashion to go naked,
Since the old Anything was created . . .

Why Should I Care for the Men of Thames

Why should I care for the men of Thames
Or the cheating waves of charter'd streams
Or shrink at the little blasts of fear
That the hireling blows into my ear

Tho born on the cheating banks of Thames
Tho his waters bathed my infant limbs
The Ohio shall wash his stains from me
I was born a slave but I go to be free.

Why Was Cupid a Boy?

Why was Cupid a boy,
And why a boy was he?
He should have been a girl,
For aught that I can see.

For he shoots with his bow,
And the girl shoots with her eye,
And they both are merry and glad,
And laugh when we do cry.

And to make Cupid a boy
Was the Cupid girl's mocking plan;
For a boy can't interpret the thing
Till he is become a man.

And then he's so pierc'd with cares,
And wounded with arrowy smarts,
That the whole business of his life
Is to pick out the heads of the darts.

'Twas the Greeks' love of war
Turn'd Love into a boy,

And woman into a statue of stone--
And away fled every joy.

You Don't Believe

You don't believe -- I won't attempt to make ye:
You are asleep -- I won't attempt to wake ye.
Sleep on! sleep on! while in your pleasant dreams
Of Reason you may drink of Life's clear streams.
Reason and Newton, they are quite two things;
For so the swallow and the sparrow sings.

Reason says `Miracle': Newton says `Doubt.'
Aye! that's the way to make all Nature out.
`Doubt, doubt, and don't believe without experiment':
That is the very thing that Jesus meant,
When He said `Only believe! believe and try!
Try, try, and never mind the reason why!'

Eternity

He who binds to himself a joy
Does the winged life destroy;
But he who kisses the joy as it flies
Lives in eternity's sun rise.

Fair Elanor

The bell struck one, and shook the silent tower;
The graves give up their dead: fair Elenor
Walk'd by the castle gate, and lookèd in.
A hollow groan ran thro' the dreary vaults,
She shriek'd aloud, and sunk upon the steps,
On the cold stone her pale cheeks. Sickly smells
Of death issue as from a sepulchre,
And all is silent but the sighing vaults.

Chill Death withdraws his hand, and she revives;
Amaz'd, she finds herself upon her feet,

And, like a ghost, thro' narrow passages
Walking, feeling the cold walls with her hands.

Fancy returns, and now she thinks of bones
And grinning skulls, and corruptible death
Wrapp'd in his shroud; and now fancies she hears
Deep sighs, and sees pale sickly ghosts gliding.

At length, no fancy but reality
Distracts her. A rushing sound, and the feet
Of one that fled, approaches--Ellen stood
Like a dumb statue, froze to stone with fear.

The wretch approaches, crying: `The deed is done;
Take this, and send it by whom thou wilt send;
It is my life--send it to Elenor:--
He's dead, and howling after me for blood!

`Take this,' he cried; and thrust into her arms
A wet napkin, wrapp'd about; then rush'd
Past, howling: she receiv'd into her arms
Pale death, and follow'd on the wings of fear.

They pass'd swift thro' the outer gate; the wretch,
Howling, leap'd o'er the wall into the moat,
Stifling in mud. Fair Ellen pass'd the bridge,
And heard a gloomy voice cry `Is it done?'

As the deer wounded, Ellen flew over
The pathless plain; as the arrows that fly
By night, destruction flies, and strikes in darkness.
She fled from fear, till at her house arriv'd.

Her maids await her; on her bed she falls,
That bed of joy, where erst her lord hath press'd:
`Ah, woman's fear!' she cried; `ah, cursèd duke!
Ah, my dear lord! ah, wretched Elenor!

`My lord was like a flower upon the brows

Of lusty May! Ah, life as frail as flower!
O ghastly death! withdraw thy cruel hand,
Seek'st thou that flow'r to deck thy horrid temples?

`My lord was like a star in highest heav'n
Drawn down to earth by spells and wickedness;
My lord was like the opening eyes of day
When western winds creep softly o'er the flowers;

`But he is darken'd; like the summer's noon
Clouded; fall'n like the stately tree, cut down;
The breath of heaven dwelt among his leaves.
O Elenor, weak woman, fill'd with woe!'

Thus having spoke, she raisèd up her head,
And saw the bloody napkin by her side,
Which in her arms she brought; and now, tenfold
More terrifièd, saw it unfold itself.

Her eyes were fix'd; the bloody cloth unfolds,
Disclosing to her sight the murder'd head
Of her dear lord, all ghastly pale, clotted
With gory blood; it groan'd, and thus it spake:

`O Elenor, I am thy husband's head,
Who, sleeping on the stones of yonder tower,
Was 'reft of life by the accursèd duke!
A hirèd villain turn'd my sleep to death!

`O Elenor, beware the cursèd duke;
O give not him thy hand, now I am dead;
He seeks thy love; who, coward, in the night,
Hirèd a villain to bereave my life.'

She sat with dead cold limbs, stiffen'd to stone;
She took the gory head up in her arms;
She kiss'd the pale lips; she had no tears to shed;
She hugg'd it to her breast, and groan'd her last.

Gwin King of Norway

Come, kings, and listen to my song:
When Gwin, the son of Nore,
Over the nations of the North
His cruel sceptre bore;
The nobles of the land did feed
Upon the hungry poor;
They tear the poor man's lamb, and drive
The needy from their door.

`The land is desolate; our wives
And children cry for bread;
Arise, and pull the tyrant down!
Let Gwin be humblèd!'

Gordred the giant rous'd himself
From sleeping in his cave;
He shook the hills, and in the clouds
The troubl'd banners wave.

Beneath them roll'd, like tempests black,
The num'rous sons of blood;
Like lions' whelps, roaring abroad,
Seeking their nightly food.

Down Bleron's hills they dreadful rush,
Their cry ascends the clouds;
The trampling horse and clanging arms
Like rushing mighty floods!

Their wives and children, weeping loud,
Follow in wild array,
Howling like ghosts, furious as wolves
In the bleak wintry day.

`Pull down the tyrant to the dust,
Let Gwin be humblèd,'
They cry, `and let ten thousand lives

Pay for the tyrant's head.'

From tow'r to tow'r the watchmen cry,
`O Gwin, the son of Nore,
Arouse thyself! the nations, black
Like clouds, come rolling o'er!'

Gwin rear'd his shield, his palace shakes,
His chiefs come rushing round;
Each, like an awful thunder cloud,
With voice of solemn sound:

Like rearèd stones around a grave
They stand around the King;
Then suddenly each seiz'd his spear,
And clashing steel does ring.

The husbandman does leave his plough
To wade thro' fields of gore;
The merchant binds his brows in steel,
And leaves the trading shore;

The shepherd leaves his mellow pipe,
And sounds the trumpet shrill;
The workman throws his hammer down
To heave the bloody bill.

Like the tall ghost of Barraton
Who sports in stormy sky,
Gwin leads his host, as black as night
When pestilence does fly,

With horses and with chariots--
And all his spearmen bold
March to the sound of mournful song,
Like clouds around him roll'd

Gwin lifts his hand--the nations halt;
`Prepare for war!' he cries--

Gordred appears!--his frowning brow
Troubles our northern skies.

The armies stand, like balances
Held in th' Almighty's hand;--
`Gwin, thou hast fill'd thy measure up:
Thou'rt swept from out the land.'

And now the raging armies rush'd
Like warring mighty seas;
The heav'ns are shook with roaring war,
The dust ascends the skies!

Earth smokes with blood, and groans and shakes
To drink her children's gore,
A sea of blood; nor can the eye
See to the trembling shore!

And on the verge of this wild sea
Famine and death doth cry;
The cries of women and of babes
Over the field doth fly.

The King is seen raging afar,
With all his men of might;
Like blazing comets scattering death
Thro' the red fev'rous night.

Beneath his arm like sheep they die,
And groan upon the plain;
The battle faints, and bloody men
Fight upon hills of slain.

Now death is sick, and riven men
Labour and toil for life;
Steed rolls on steed, and shield on shield,
Sunk in this sea of strife!

The god of war is drunk with blood;

The earth doth faint and fail;
The stench of blood makes sick the heav'ns;
Ghosts glut the throat of hell!

O what have kings to answer for
Before that awful throne;
When thousand deaths for vengeance cry,
And ghosts accusing groan!

Like blazing comets in the sky
That shake the stars of light,
Which drop like fruit unto the earth
Thro' the fierce burning night;

Like these did Gwin and Gordred meet,
And the first blow decides;
Down from the brow unto the breast
Gordred his head divides!

Gwin fell: the sons of Norway fled,
All that remain'd alive;
The rest did fill the vale of death,
For them the eagles strive.

The river Dorman roll'd their blood
Into the northern sea;
Who mourn'd his sons, and overwhelm'd
The pleasant south country.

How Sweet I Roam'd

How sweet I roam'd from field to field,
And tasted all the summer's pride
'Til the prince of love beheld
Who in the sunny beams did glide!

He shew'd me lilies for my hair
And blushing roses for my brow;
He led me through his garden fair,

Where all his golden pleasures grow.

With sweet May dews my wings were wet,
And Phoebus fir'd my vocal rage
He caught me in his silken net,
And shut me in his golden cage.

He loves to sit and hear me sing,
Then, laughing, sports and plays with me;
Then stretches out my golden wing,
And mocks my loss of liberty.

I Heard an Angel

I heard an Angel singing
When the day was springing,
'Mercy, Pity, Peace
Is the world's release.'

Thus he sung all day
Over the new mown hay,
Till the sun went down
And haycocks looked brown.

I heard a Devil curse
Over the heath and the furze,
'Mercy could be no more,
If there was nobody poor,

And pity no more could be,
If all were as happy as we.'
At his curse the sun went down,
And the heavens gave a frown.

Down pour'd the heavy rain
Over the new reap'd grain ...
And Miseries' increase
Is Mercy, Pity, Peace.

I Rose Up at the Dawn of Day

I rose up at the dawn of day--
`Get thee away! get thee away!
Pray'st thou for riches? Away! away!
This is the Throne of Mammon grey.'

Said I: This, sure, is very odd;
I took it to be the Throne of God.
For everything besides I have:
It is only for riches that I can crave.

I have mental joy, and mental health,
And mental friends, and mental wealth;
I've a wife I love, and that loves me;
I've all but riches bodily.

I am in God's presence night and day,
And He never turns His face away;
The accuser of sins by my side doth stand,
And he holds my money-bag in his hand.

For my worldly things God makes him pay,
And he'd pay for more if to him I would pray;
And so you may do the worst you can do;
Be assur'd, Mr. Devil, I won't pray to you.

Then if for riches I must not pray,
God knows, I little of prayers need say;
So, as a church is known by its steeple,
If I pray it must be for other people.

He says, if I do not worship him for a God,
I shall eat coarser food, and go worse shod;
So, as I don't value such things as these,
You must do, Mr. Devil, just as God please.

I Saw a Chapel

I saw a chapel all of gold
That none did dare to enter in,
And many weeping stood without,
Weeping, mourning, worshipping.

I saw a serpent rise between
The white pillars of the door,
And he forc'd and forc'd and forc'd,
Down the golden hinges tore.

And along the pavement sweet,
Set with pearls and rubies bright,
All his slimy length he drew
Till upon the altar white

Vomiting his poison out
On the bread and on the wine.
So I turn'd into a sty
And laid me down among the swine.

I see the Four-fold Man

I see the Four-fold Man, The Humanity in deadly sleep
And its fallen Emanation, the Spectre and its cruel Shadow.
I see the Past, Present and Future existing all at once
Before me. O Divine Spirit, sustain me on thy wings,
That I may awake Albion from his long and cold repose;
For Bacon and Newton, sheath'd in dismal steel, their terrors hang
Like iron scourges over Albion: reasonings like vast serpents
Infold around my limbs, bruising my minute articulations.

I turn my eyes to the schools and universities of Europe
And there behold the Loom of Locke, whose Woof rages dire,
Wash'd by the Water-wheels of Newton: black the cloth
In heavy wreaths folds over every nation: cruel works
Of many Wheels I view, wheel without wheel, with cogs tyrannic

Moving by compulsion each other, not as those in Eden, which,
Wheel within wheel, in freedom revolve in harmony and peace.

If It Is True What the Prophets Write

If it is true, what the Prophets write,
That the heathen gods are all stocks and stones,
Shall we, for the sake of being polite,
Feed them with the juice of our marrow-bones?

And if Bezaleel and Aholiab drew
What the finger of God pointed to their view,
Shall we suffer the Roman and Grecian rods
To compel us to worship them as gods?

They stole them from the temple of the Lord
And worshipp'd them that they might make inspirèd art abhorr'd;

The wood and stone were call'd the holy things,
And their sublime intent given to their kings.
All the atonements of Jehovah spurn'd,
And criminals to sacrifices turn'd.

Several Questions Answered

What is it men in women do require?
The lineaments of Gratified Desire.
What is it women do in men require?
The lineaments of Gratified Desire.

The look of love alarms
Because 'tis fill'd with fire;
But the look of soft deceit
Shall Win the lover's hire.

Soft Deceit & Idleness,
These are Beauty's sweetest dress.

Silent, Silent Night

Silent, silent night,
Quench the holy light
Of thy torches bright;

For possessed of Day
Thousand spirits stray
That sweet joys betray.

Why should joys be sweet
Used with deceit,
Nor with sorrows meet?

But an honest joy
Does itself destroy
For a harlot coy.

Sleep! Sleep! Beauty Bright

Sleep! sleep! beauty bright,
Dreaming o'er the joys of night;
Sleep! sleep! in thy sleep
Little sorrows sit and weep.

Sweet Babe, in thy face
Soft desires I can trace,
Secret joys and secret smiles,
Little pretty infant wiles.

As thy softest limbs I feel,
Smiles as of the morning steal
O'er thy cheek, and o'er thy breast
Where thy little breast does rest.

O! the cunning wiles that creep
In thy little heart asleep.
When thy little heart does wake
Then the dreadful lightnings break,

From thy cheek and from thy eye,
O'er the youthful harvests nigh.
Infant wiles and infant smiles
Heaven and Earth of peace beguiles.

Song

My silks and fine array,
My smiles and languish'd air,
By love are driv'n away;
And mournful lean Despair
Brings me yew to deck my grave;
Such end true lovers have.

His face is fair as heav'n
When springing buds unfold;
O why to him was't giv'n
Whose heart is wintry cold?
His breast is love's all-worshipp'd tomb,
Where all love's pilgrims come.

Bring me an axe and spade,
Bring me a winding sheet;
When I my grave have made
Let winds and tempests beat:
Then down I'll lie as cold as clay.
True love doth pass away!

The Angel that presided o'er my birth

The Angel that presided o'er my birth
Said, 'Little creature, form'd of Joy and Mirth,
'Go love without the help of any Thing on Earth.'

The Birds

He: Where thou dwellest, in what grove,
Tell me Fair One, tell me Love;
Where thou thy charming nest dost build,
O thou pride of every field!

She: Yonder stands a lonely tree,
There I live and mourn for thee;
Morning drinks my silent tear,
And evening winds my sorrow bear.

He: O thou summer's harmony,
I have liv'd and mourn'd for thee;
Each day I mourn along the wood,
And night hath heard my sorrows loud.

She: Dost thou truly long for me?
And am I thus sweet to thee?
Sorrow now is at an end,
O my Lover and my Friend!

He: Come, on wings of joy we'll fly
To where my bower hangs on high;
Come, and make thy calm retreat
Among green leaves and blossoms sweet.

The Land of Dreams

Awake, awake, my little boy!
Thou wast thy mother's only joy;
Why dost thou weep in thy gentle sleep?
Awake! thy father does thee keep.

'O, what land is the Land of Dreams?
What are its mountains, and what are its streams?
O father! I saw my mother there,

Among the lilies by waters fair.

'Among the lambs, cloth?d in white,
She walk'd with her Thomas in sweet delight.
I wept for joy, like a dove I mourn;
O! when shall I again return?'

Dear child, I also by pleasant streams
Have wander'd all night in the Land of Dreams;
But tho' calm and warm the waters wide,
I could not get to the other side.

'Father, O father! what do we here
In this land of unbelief and fear?
The Land of Dreams is better far
Above the light of the morning star.'

The Two Songs

I heard an Angel Singing
When the day was springing:
"Mercy, pity, and peace,
Are the world's release."

So he sang all day
Over the new-mown hay,
Till the sun went down,
And the haycocks looked brown.

I heard a devil curse
Over the heath and the furse:
"Mercy vould be no more
If there were nobody poor,
And pity no more could be
If all were happy as ye:
And mutual fear brings peace,
Misery's increase
Are mercy, pity, and peace."

At his curse the sun went down,
And the heavens gave a frown.

The Caverns of the Graves I've Seen

The Caverns of the Grave I've seen,
And these I show'd to England's Queen.
But now the Caves of Hell I view,
Who shall I dare to show them to?
What mighty soul in Beauty's form
Shall dauntless view the infernal storm?
Egremont's Countess can control
The flames of Hell that round me roll;
If she refuse, I still go on
Till the Heavens and Earth are gone,
Still admir'd by noble minds,
Follow'd by Envy on the winds,
Re-engrav'd time after time,
Ever in their youthful prime,
My designs unchang'd remain.
Time may rage, but rage in vain.
For above Time's troubled fountains,
On the great Atlantic Mountains,
In my Golden House on high,
There they shine eternally.

The Crystal Cabinet

The Maiden caught me in the wild,
Where I was dancing merrily;
She put me into her Cabinet,
And lock'd me up with a golden key.

This cabinet is form'd of gold
And pearl and crystal shining bright,
And within it opens into a world
And a little lovely moony night.

Another England there I saw
Another London with its Tower,
Another Thames and other hills,
And another pleasant Surrey bower.

Another Maiden like herself,
Translucent, lovely, shining clear,
Threefold each in the other clos'd
O, what a pleasant trembling fear!

O, what a smile! a threefold smile
Fill'd me, that like a flame I burn'd;
I bent to kiss the lovely Maid,
And found a threefold kiss return'd.

I strove to seize the inmost form
With ardor fierce and hands of flame,
But burst the Crystal Cabinet,
And like a weeping Babe became--

A weeping Babe upon the wild,
And weeping Woman pale reclin'd,
And in the outward air again,
I fill'd with woes the passing wind.

The Everlasting Gospel

The vision of Christ that thou dost see
Is my vision's greatest enemy.
Thine has a great hook nose like thine;
Mine has a snub nose like to mine.
Thine is the Friend of all Mankind;
Mine speaks in parables to the blind.
Thine loves the same world that mine hates;
Thy heaven doors are my hell gates.
Socrates taught what Meletus
Loath'd as a nation's bitterest curse,
And Caiaphas was in his own mind
A benefactor to mankind.

Both read the Bible day and night,
But thou read'st black where I read white.

Was Jesus gentle, or did He
Give any marks of gentility?
When twelve years old He ran away,
And left His parents in dismay.
When after three days' sorrow found,
Loud as Sinai's trumpet-sound:
'No earthly parents I confess—
My Heavenly Father's business!!
Ye understand not what I say,
And, angry, force Me to obey.
Obedience is a duty then,
And favour gains with God and men.'
John from the wilderness loud cried;
Satan gloried in his pride.
'Come,' said Satan, 'come away,
I'll soon see if you'll obey!
John for disobedience bled,
But you can turn the stones to bread.
God's high king and God's high priest
Shall plant their glories in your breast,
If Caiaphas you will obey,
If Herod you with bloody prey
Feed with the sacrifice, and be
Obedient, fall down, worship me.'
Thunders and lightnings broke around,
And Jesus' voice in thunders' sound:
'Thus I seize the spiritual prey.
Ye smiters with disease, make way.
I come your King and God to seize,
Is God a smiter with disease?'
The God of this world rag'd in vain:
He bound old Satan in His chain,
And, bursting forth, His furious ire
Became a chariot of fire.
Throughout the land He took His course,
And trac'd diseases to their source.

He curs'd the Scribe and Pharisee,
Trampling down hypocrisy.
Where'er His chariot took its way,
There Gates of Death let in the Day,
Broke down from every chain and bar;
And Satan in His spiritual war
Dragg'd at His chariot-wheels: loud howl'd
The God of this world: louder roll'd
The chariot-wheels, and louder still
His voice was heard from Zion's Hill,
And in His hand the scourge shone bright;
He scourg'd the merchant Canaanite
From out the Temple of His Mind,
And in his body tight does bind
Satan and all his hellish crew;
And thus with wrath He did subdue
The serpent bulk of Nature's dross,
Till He had nail'd it to the Cross.
He took on sin in the Virgin's womb
And put it off on the Cross and tomb
To be worshipp'd by the Church of Rome.

Was Jesus humble? or did He
Give any proofs of humility?
Boast of high things with humble tone,
And give with charity a stone?
When but a child He ran away,
And left His parents in dismay.
When they had wander'd three days long
These were the words upon His tongue:
'No earthly parents I confess:
I am doing My Father's business.'
When the rich learnèd Pharisee
Came to consult Him secretly,
Upon his heart with iron pen
He wrote 'Ye must be born again.'
He was too proud to take a bribe;
He spoke with authority, not like a Scribe.
He says with most consummate art

'Follow Me, I am meek and lowly of heart,
As that is the only way to escape
The miser's net and the glutton's trap.'
What can be done with such desperate fools
Who follow after the heathen schools?
I was standing by when Jesus died;
What I call'd humility, they call'd pride.
He who loves his enemies betrays his friends.
This surely is not what Jesus intends;
But the sneaking pride of heroic schools,
And the Scribes' and Pharisees' virtuous rules;
For He acts with honest, triumphant pride,
And this is the cause that Jesus dies.
He did not die with Christian ease,
Asking pardon of His enemies:
If He had, Caiaphas would forgive;
Sneaking submission can always live.
He had only to say that God was the Devil,
And the Devil was God, like a Christian civil;
Mild Christian regrets to the Devil confess
For affronting him thrice in the wilderness;
He had soon been bloody Caesar's elf,
And at last he would have been Caesar himself,
Like Dr. Priestly and Bacon and Newton—
Poor spiritual knowledge is not worth a button
For thus the Gospel Sir Isaac confutes:
'God can only be known by His attributes;
And as for the indwelling of the Holy Ghost,
Or of Christ and His Father, it's all a boast
And pride, and vanity of the imagination,
That disdains to follow this world's fashion.'
To teach doubt and experiment
Certainly was not what Christ meant.
What was He doing all that time,
From twelve years old to manly prime?
Was He then idle, or the less
About His Father's business?
Or was His wisdom held in scorn
Before His wrath began to burn

In miracles throughout the land,
That quite unnerv'd the Seraph band?
If He had been Antichrist, Creeping Jesus,
He'd have done anything to please us;
Gone sneaking into synagogues,
And not us'd the Elders and Priests like dogs;
But humble as a lamb or ass
Obey'd Himself to Caiaphas.
God wants not man to humble himself:
That is the trick of the Ancient Elf.
This is the race that Jesus ran:
Humble to God, haughty to man,
Cursing the Rulers before the people
Even to the Temple's highest steeple,
And when He humbled Himself to God
Then descended the cruel rod.
'If Thou Humblest Thyself, Thou humblest Me.
Thou also dwell'st in Eternity.
Thou art a Man: God is no more:
Thy own Humanity learn to adore,
For that is My spirit of life.
Awake, arise to spiritual strife,
And Thy revenge abroad display
In terrors at the last Judgement Day.
God's mercy and long suffering
Is but the sinner to judgement to bring.
Thou on the Cross for them shalt pray—
And take revenge at the Last Day.'
Jesus replied, and thunders hurl'd:
'I never will pray for the world.
Once I did so when I pray'd in the Garden;
I wish'd to take with Me a bodily pardon.'
Can that which was of woman born,
In the absence of the morn,
When the Soul fell into sleep,
And Archangels round it weep,
Shooting out against the light
Fibres of a deadly night,
Reasoning upon its own dark fiction,

In doubt which is self-contradiction?
Humility is only doubt,
And does the sun and moon blot out,
Rooting over with thorns and stems
The buried soul and all its gems.
This life's five windows of the soul
Distorts the Heavens from pole to pole,
And leads you to believe a lie
When you see with, not thro', the eye
That was born in a night, to perish in a night,
When the soul slept in the beams of light.

Did Jesus teach doubt? or did He
Give any lessons of philosophy,
Charge Visionaries with deceiving,
Or call men wise for not believing?...

Was Jesus born of a Virgin pure
With narrow soul and looks demure?
If He intended to take on sin
The Mother should an harlot been,
Just such a one as Magdalen,
With seven devils in her pen.
Or were Jew virgins still more curs'd,
And more sucking devils nurs'd?
Or what was it which He took on
That He might bring salvation?
A body subject to be tempted,
From neither pain nor grief exempted;
Or such a body as might not feel
The passions that with sinners deal?
Yes, but they say He never fell.
Ask Caiaphas; for he can tell.—
'He mock'd the Sabbath, and He mock'd
The Sabbath's God, and He unlock'd
The evil spirits from their shrines,
And turn'd fishermen to divines;
O'erturn'd the tent of secret sins,
And its golden cords and pins,

In the bloody shrine of war
Pour'd around from star to star,—
Halls of justice, hating vice,
Where the Devil combs his lice.
He turn'd the devils into swine
That He might tempt the Jews to dine;
Since which, a pig has got a look
That for a Jew may be mistook.
"Obey your parents."—What says He?
"Woman, what have I to do with thee?
No earthly parents I confess:
I am doing my Father's business."
He scorn'd Earth's parents, scorn'd Earth's God,
And mock'd the one and the other's rod;
His seventy Disciples sent
Against Religion and Government—
They by the sword of Justice fell,
And Him their cruel murderer tell.
He left His father's trade to roam,
A wand'ring vagrant without home;
And thus He others' labour stole,
That He might live above control.
The publicans and harlots He
Selected for His company,
And from the adulteress turn'd away
God's righteous law, that lost its prey.'
Was Jesus chaste? or did He
Give any lessons of chastity?
The Morning blushèd fiery red:
Mary was found in adulterous bed;
Earth groan'd beneath, and Heaven above
Trembled at discovery of Love.
Jesus was sitting in Moses' chair.
They brought the trembling woman there.
Moses commands she be ston'd to death.
What was the sound of Jesus' breath?
He laid His hand on Moses' law;
The ancient Heavens, in silent awe,
Writ with curses from pole to pole,

All away began to roll.
The Earth trembling and naked lay
In secret bed of mortal clay;
On Sinai felt the Hand Divine
Pulling back the bloody shrine;
And she heard the breath of God,
As she heard by Eden's flood:
'Good and Evil are no more!
Sinai's trumpets cease to roar!
Cease, finger of God, to write!
The Heavens are not clean in Thy sight.
Thou art good, and Thou alone;
Nor may the sinner cast one stone.
To be good only, is to be
A God or else a Pharisee.
Thou Angel of the Presence Divine,
That didst create this Body of Mine,
Wherefore hast thou writ these laws
And created Hell's dark jaws?
My Presence I will take from thee:
A cold leper thou shalt be.
Tho' thou wast so pure and bright
That Heaven was impure in thy sight,
Tho' thy oath turn'd Heaven pale,
Tho' thy covenant built Hell's jail,
Tho' thou didst all to chaos roll
With the Serpent for its soul,
Still the breath Divine does move,
And the breath Divine is Love.
Mary, fear not! Let me see
The seven devils that torment thee.
Hide not from My sight thy sin,
That forgiveness thou may'st win.
Has no man condemnèd thee?'
'No man, Lord.' 'Then what is he
Who shall accuse thee? Come ye forth,
Fallen fiends of heavenly birth,
That have forgot your ancient love,
And driven away my trembling Dove.

You shall bow before her feet;
You shall lick the dust for meat;
And tho' you cannot love, but hate,
Shall be beggars at Love's gate.
What was thy love? Let Me see it;
Was it love or dark deceit?'
'Love too long from me has fled;
'Twas dark deceit, to earn my bread;
'Twas covet, or 'twas custom, or
Some trifle not worth caring for;
That they may call a shame and sin
Love's temple that God dwelleth in,
And hide in secret hidden shrine
The naked Human Form Divine,
And render that a lawless thing
On which the Soul expands its wing.
But this, O Lord, this was my sin,
When first I let these devils in,
In dark pretence to chastity
Blaspheming Love, blaspheming Thee,
Thence rose secret adulteries,
And thence did covet also rise.
My sin Thou hast forgiven me;
Canst Thou forgive my blasphemy?
Canst Thou return to this dark hell,
And in my burning bosom dwell?
And canst Thou die that I may live?
And canst Thou pity and forgive?'
Then roll'd the shadowy Man away
From the limbs of Jesus, to make them His prey,
An ever devouring appetite,
Glittering with festering venoms bright;
Crying 'Crucify this cause of distress,
Who don't keep the secrets of holiness!
The mental powers by diseases we bind;
But He heals the deaf, the dumb, and the blind.
Whom God has afflicted for secret ends,
He comforts and heals and calls them friends.'
But, when Jesus was crucified,

Then was perfected His galling pride.
In three nights He devour'd His prey,
And still He devours the body of clay;
For dust and clay is the Serpent's meat,
Which never was made for Man to eat.

Seeing this False Christ, in fury and passion
I made my voice heard all over the nation.
What are those…

I am sure this Jesus will not do,
Either for Englishman or Jew

The Grey Monk

'I die, I die!' the Mother said,
'My children die for lack of bread.
What more has the merciless Tyrant said?'
The Monk sat down on the stony bed.

The blood red ran from the Grey Monk's side,
His hands and feet were wounded wide,
His body bent, his arms and knees
Like to the roots of ancient trees.

His eye was dry; no tear could flow:
A hollow groan first spoke his woe.
He trembled and shudder'd upon the bed;
At length with a feeble cry he said:

'When God commanded this hand to write
In the studious hours of deep midnight,
He told me the writing I wrote should prove
The bane of all that on Earth I lov'd.

My Brother starv'd between two walls,
His Children's cry my soul appalls;
I mock'd at the rack and griding chain,
My bent body mocks their torturing pain.

Thy father drew his sword in the North,
With his thousands strong he marched forth;
Thy Brother has arm'd himself in steel
To avenge the wrongs thy Children feel.

But vain the Sword and vain the Bow,
They never can work War's overthrow.
The Hermit's prayer and the Widow's tear
Alone can free the World from fear.

For a Tear is an intellectual thing,
And a Sigh is the sword of an Angel King,
And the bitter groan of the Martyr's woe
Is an arrow from the Almighty's bow.

The hand of Vengeance found the bed
To which the Purple Tyrant fled;
The iron hand crush'd the Tyrant's head
And became a Tyrant in his stead.'

Printed in Great Britain
by Amazon